This book is primarily a work of fiction. The names, characters, places and incidents are based on the author's imagination. Financial concepts are based on fact and the author's opinion.

First paperback edition 2018

ISBN 978-0-9977910-4-4 (paperback)

Eleven Digital Group, LLC
New York, NY
info@elevendigitalgroup.com

Visit us at bullbearkidsbooks.com

Adventures in Finance with Bull & Bear

Borrowing for New Bikes

Created By: Roy & Susan Kim

Illustrated By: Surendhra K. Padayatchi

To Addison and Alexis

Bull and Bear were in the store looking at new bikes.

They were amazed by the selection, but jaws dropped when they saw the price.

A salesman spotted disappointment
and rushed to help them out.
CITY
BIKES
He said, "Please
tell me what
is bothering you...
... so we can flip those
frowns around."

Bear said, "These bikes cost too much. I'm afraid we'll have to leave."

The salesman smiled and said, "I have a deal you won't believe!"

The salesman said that with a loan
they could leave with bikes today.
Bull and Bear were so excited they
didn't know what to say.

Bull and Bear signed papers, then the
salesman said "off you go!"
Because of their excitement, they
forgot to ask, "what's a loan?"

The bikes were
used every day...

...for school, work,
and of course fun!

They raced around the neighborhood
every second there was sun.

Bull liked doing crazy tricks and
jumps all over the place.

Bear liked riding fast and
feeling the wind on her face.

Weeks passed and Bear got a bill. She almost dropped to the floor! Bull came out yelling minutes later...
"DID YOU GET THIS LETTER FROM THE STORE!?"

Bull and Bear owed a lot of money...
...SO MUCH that they were confused.
They were embarrassed and felt lied to. This was not great news.

Bull asked, "Why do we owe so much money?! I mean seriously why so much!"
Bear replied...
"I knew the deal was too good to be true. I also have questions - a bunch!"

Bear did what she should have first
and researched loans on the net.
She learned they borrowed money,
and must repay their debt.

Bear explained, "Loans come with something called interest, so this money is not free. What we owe will keep growing, and could become a problem for you and me."

Bull kicked and screamed and cried out loud - he was very mad. Bear calmly laid out a plan - for this they were both glad.

They paid off part of what they owed, and needed a plan for the rest. Bull shouted, "I have an idea that is absolutely the best!"

Bull explained, "We can put on a live show here in the city...

... and sell lots of tickets

... to friends and family."

Bull continued, "I can use my bike to do tricks for the fans.
Bear... You can manage the money and all the business plans."

Bear didn't like admitting it, but Bull's idea was the best.

They earned enough to pay off their debt. The show was a huge success.

When you come across a deal that seems too good to be true, you are probably right so be careful what you do.

Remember, when you buy something with a loan the money isn't free. It's important when you get a loan you do so responsibly.

Don't miss the other adventures in our series...

Visit us at BullBearKidsBooks.com

Money Activities

Hey kids! Here are some activities to help you learn more about money and borrowing. On the next few pages you'll find matching games, word searches, puzzles and more for you to enjoy.

When you finish these activities, ask your parents to help you visit the Bull & Bear Academy at BullBearKidsBooks.com for more **FREE** activities.

MONEY MATCH

Instructions:
First, look at the words and the coins. Draw a line to match a word to the correct coin. Next, look at the coins and the values. Draw a line to match a coin and the correct value.

Words	**Coins**	**Values**
Penny		**$0.05** **5¢**
Quarter		**$0.25** **25¢**
Dime		**$0.01** **1¢**
Nickel		**$0.10** **10¢**

WORD SEARCH

Instructions:
Search for the words in the list below. Circle a word when you find it. Have fun!

List:

Loan	Bank	Principal
Debt	Loan Officer	Default
Borrower	Mortgage	Credit Score
Interest	Payment	Maturity

A	Z	X	L	S	T	Y	F	O	P	R	P	L	V
C	B	N	M	R	D	H	Y	P	W	G	Q	O	V
G	T	S	E	R	E	T	N	I	J	X	R	A	P
F	R	I	H	U	J	O	T	P	I	O	D	N	V
R	H	C	I	O	I	L	U	Y	O	P	W	O	Q
P	Q	W	E	R	U	T	Y	U	I	O	P	F	A
S	D	F	G	A	H	J	K	L	Z	X	C	F	V
B	N	M	F	Q	W	B	E	R	T	Y	U	I	I
O	P	E	A	S	L	O	A	N	D	F	G	C	H
J	D	K	Y	L	Z	X	C	N	V	B	N	E	M
L	Q	W	E	R	T	Y	U	I	K	O	E	R	P
A	A	S	I	D	F	G	H	T	J	K	R	L	Z
P	X	C	R	V	B	N	M	N	Q	W	O	E	R
I	T	Y	U	U	O	P	R	E	A	S	C	D	F
C	G	H	T	J	K	E	L	M	Z	X	S	C	V
N	M	Q	A	W	W	E	R	Y	T	Y	T	U	I
I	O	P	M	O	R	T	G	A	G	E	I	A	S
R	D	F	R	G	H	J	K	P	L	Z	D	X	D
P	C	R	V	B	N	M	Q	W	E	R	E	T	E
U	O	I	O	P	A	S	D	F	G	H	R	J	B
B	K	L	Z	X	C	V	B	N	M	Q	C	W	T

WORD SEARCH

Instructions:
Search for the words in the list below. Circle a word when you find it. Have fun!

List:

APR
Consolidation
Delinquent
Guarantor
Note
Student Loan
Credit Card
Lender
CFPB
FDIC
OCC
Debt To Income

Q	W	R	V	Z	N	K	I	F	A	H	O	P	X
K	Q	N	M	D	J	A	N	U	S	M	G	G	B
Q	T	A	V	Y	U	N	X	Z	R	U	R	O	M
W	G	Y	P	H	K	N	X	C	I	E	T	C	V
P	H	E	Y	R	A	Q	T	H	D	H	V	X	T
H	K	T	I	Z	B	M	Q	N	X	C	G	R	U
S	Q	W	F	H	J	K	E	R	U	B	O	V	T
T	C	O	N	S	O	L	I	D	A	T	I	O	N
U	P	O	X	T	U	M	X	Q	N	Y	C	C	E
D	T	P	F	Q	E	N	A	A	I	C	O	G	U
E	H	U	T	I	K	L	R	F	U	A	N	T	Q
N	R	O	Y	F	N	A	W	T	K	A	U	N	N
T	C	N	T	I	U	Q	F	R	N	M	C	Z	I
L	O	K	L	G	U	R	T	J	L	S	B	V	L
O	H	I	Z	W	J	I	L	P	B	G	F	X	E
A	T	J	M	N	C	W	Y	G	S	H	T	U	D
N	P	K	F	I	O	B	E	T	Y	K	A	G	Y
L	Z	D	V	T	J	P	A	T	J	L	C	C	X
P	I	E	R	Y	I	F	E	L	F	T	H	N	Q
C	R	E	D	I	T	C	A	R	D	H	E	L	O
D	E	B	T	T	O	I	N	C	O	M	E	D	G

SECRET MESSAGE

Instructions:
Use the decoder below to read the secret message.

Legend:

A	B	C	D	E	F	G	H	I	J	K	L	M
1	2	3	4	5	6	7	8	9	10	11	12	13

N	O	P	Q	R	S	T	U	V	W	X	Y	Z
14	15	16	17	18	19	20	21	22	23	24	25	26

Secret Message:

8	5	12	12	15

11	9	4	19

.

25	15	21

3	18	1	3	11	5	4

20	8	5

19	5	3	18	5	20

3	15	4	5

.

			'	
4	15	14		20

2	15	18	18	15	23

21	14	12	5	19	19

25	15	21

3	1	14

16	1	25

9	20

2	1	3	11

.

SECRET MESSAGE

Instructions:
Use the decoder below to read the secret message.

Legend:

A	B	C	D	E	F	G	H	I	J	K	L	M
1	2	3	4	5	6	7	8	9	10	11	12	13

N	O	P	Q	R	S	T	U	V	W	X	Y	Z
14	15	16	17	18	19	20	21	22	23	24	25	26

Secret Message:

12	15	1	14	19

3	1	14

2	5

5	1	19	25

20	15

7	5	20

,

2	21	20

8	1	18	4

20	15

16	1	25

2	1	3	11

.

13	1	11	5

19	21	18	5

20	15

2	15	18	18	15	23

18	5	19	16	15	14	19	9	2	12	25

.

HOW MANY WORDS?

Instructions:
Look at the word provided below and see how many different words you can come up with. Write your words in the box provided.

Word:

MORTGAGE

Other Words:

HOW MANY WORDS?

Instructions:
Look at the word provided below and see how many different words you can come up with. Write your words in the box provided.

Word:

STUDENT LOAN

Other Words:

WORD PROBLEMS

Instructions:
Solve the following word problems using the facts provided. Each question is more difficult than the last so good luck!

Word Problems:

1. Susan borrowed $10 from a friend. Susan paid back $8 so far. How much does Susan owe her friend?

2. Ellie borrowed $20 from Alexis. Ellie paid back $10 one week then $5 the next week. How much does Ellie still owe Alexis?

3. Tony loaned his friend $100. Tony's friend paid back $50. How much money does Tony's friend still owe?

4. Mark loaned Joe $25. Joe borrowed another $10 from Ben, and $5 from Alexis. How much does Joe owe?

5. Alexis needs a new bike for her job. She finds a used bike in good condition that costs $200. She has $150 in cash to buy the bike. How much does Alexis need to borrow from mom and dad to buy the bike?

6. Addison borrowed money that was due last month. She owed $50. Interest of $10 is charged if loans are not paid in full by the due date. Also, if payments are late the bank charges a $100 fee. How much does Addison now owe for being late on her payment? (HINT: Amount owed = Payment Due + Interest and Fees)

Made in United States
Orlando, FL
04 November 2026

90203669R00024